simply
Italian

© 2002 Silverback Books, San Francisco
© Photography and recipes courtesy Graefe
und Unzer Verlag GmbH, Munich and
Lisa Keenan Photography, Emeryville, CA.

Editor: Kelsey Lane
Layout and typesetting: Patty Holden
Cover: Patty Holden
Copy editing: Elizabeth Penn
Index preparation: Jonathan Silverman

Printed in Hong Kong

ISBN 1-930603-28-2

Nutritional analysis computations
are approximate.

Table of Contents

Many believe Italian food to be the darling of world cuisine, a popular force pervading countries around the globe. Of course, the United States is one of its biggest fans, in a long-standing love affair with all things Italian—pizza, Parmigiano-reggiano cheese, and cold-pressed extra virgin olive oil. But even countries such as Germany and Japan can't help but put Italy's creations high on their gastronomic lists.

The reason, we believe, revolves around three unwritten tenets of the Italian way.

First off, the Italians have long relied on fresh, local ingredients to inspire everyday meals. A garden-harvested zucchini might be roasted and then dressed only with a thin veil of olive oil to allow the full flavor of the vegetable to shine through.

And then there's the Italian penchant for dishes that are simple to prepare and unpretentious in nature. That's why the title of this book, *Simply Italian*, rings so true. Guests at an Italian dinner table need not put on airs. Though the cuisine draws from many other traditions, including French, Arab, and Grecian, the country has managed to hone their national culinary treasures into perfected dishes the world cannot resist. Think creamy and toothsome risotto, savory polenta, and rich gelato. Ponder pasta and its infinite iterations.

Finally, people never seem to tire of the Italian formula. It just plain works—satisfying dishes that can be enjoyed repeatedly, day in, day out, and through the seasons.

Much of our everyday inspiration for cooking we owe to the sensual sights, sounds, smells, and tastes of Italian cuisine.

Leafing through this cookbook, and cooking from the recipes, you'll find a broad sampling of the country's staple dishes. Bring a little of Italy's exuberant culture into your own kitchen, and enjoy.

Antipasti and Vegetables

Antipasti are simply the very beginning of an Italian meal. For instance, the most important and largest culinary spread of an Italian's day is lunch—a multi-course meal that extends into most of the afternoon. Everything shuts down for this refreshing, social event. An antipasto is served first—it need only be something small and delicious to ignite the senses as the eating gets revved up.

Vegetables are often part of the antipasti course, but also show up all throughout an Italian meal. Produce is featured in its own course, the contorno, served before the insalata and fruit toward the end of the meal. The country's peninsula is largely farmed with vegetables and grains, not primarily with cattle nor other animals—thus the focus on nature's healthiest ingredients.

Marinated Bell Peppers

Serves 4:
2 red bell peppers
2 yellow bell peppers
2 cloves garlic
1 tablespoon fresh lemon juice
2 tablespoons cold-pressed extra virgin olive oil
Salt (preferably kosher or sea)
Freshly ground black pepper
¼ cup parsley sprigs

Prep time: 45 minutes
(+ 4 hours marinating time)
Per serving approx: 96 calories
1 g protein/ 7 g fat/ 9 g carbohydrates

Set oven to 475°F. Rinse bell peppers and cut in half lengthwise through the stem. Then cut out stems and pull out interior, including seeds and ribs. Place pepper halves on a greased baking sheet with the cut sides down.

Bake peppers for about 15 minutes or until the peels have blistered and are completely black in some places; remove from oven. Wet a dish towel under cold water, squeeze it out, and lay it over the peppers. Cool peppers to room temperature.

Reserve liquid from the baking dish. Pierce blisters and slip peels off the peppers—it's fine if some traces remain. Cut peppers into strips and place in a shallow bowl with the reserved pepper liquid. Roasting and peeling in this manner brings out the fullest flavor potential, but if you're short on time, omit those steps and sauté in 1–2 tablespoons olive oil; then marinate as follows.

Peel garlic and slice cloves very thinly, then cut into fine strips. Combine with lemon juice, oil, and salt and pepper to taste; pour over the bell peppers. Marinate at least 4 hours at room temperature, stirring occasionally, and once right before serving. Last minute: rinse parsley, shake dry, mince, and sprinkle over peppers.

Serves 4:
¼ cup basil sprigs
3–4 ripe tomatoes
3 tablespoons extra virgin olive oil
Salt (preferably kosher or sea)
Freshly ground black pepper
4 large round slices Italian white bread, halved
4 cloves garlic

Prep time: 20 minutes
Per serving approx: 205 calories
3 g protein/15 g fat/17 g carbohydrates

Remove basil leaves from stems and cut into fine strips. Dice tomatoes. Mix tomatoes and basil with oil, and season with salt and pepper to taste.

Toast the bread slice halves in a toaster or in a very hot oven (about 4 minutes).

In the meantime, peel garlic. Rub into the hot, crispy bread (the bread works like a grater). Top with tomato-basil mixture and enjoy immediately.

Crostini

with Green Olive Tapenade

Serves 4:

½ cup basil sprigs
¾ cup imported green olives, pitted
1 dried red chile or crushed red pepper flakes to taste
1 tablespoon pine nuts, plus more for garnish
2 tablespoons olive oil
12 sliced bread rounds, small

Prep time: 20 minutes
Per serving approx: 312 calories
8 g protein/13 g fat/42 g carbohydrates

Rinse basil and remove leaves. Purée finely together with olives, red chile (seeds removed for less spice—or use flakes), pine nuts, and oil (using blender or hand blender). No need for salt—the olives are salty enough.

Toast bread slices in a toaster or in a very hot oven (for about 4 minutes). Spread with green olive tapenade, garnish with pine nuts, and enjoy.

Serves 4–6:
¾ pound squid fillets (and tentacles, if desired)
Salt (preferably kosher or sea)
¾ pound *cooked* peeled shrimp
1 stalk celery
1 carrot
½ cup parsley sprigs
2 tablespoons fresh lemon juice
Freshly ground black pepper
¼ cup extra virgin olive oil
1 lemon cut into wedges for serving on the side

Prep time: 30 minutes
(+ 2 hours marinating)
Per serving (6) approx: 201 calories
21 g protein/11 g fat/4 g carbohydrates

Rinse squid well under cold running water; drain. Bring salted water to a boil. Add squid and boil for 1 minute—no longer, or it will become tough. (If frozen squid, prepare according to package directions).

Place squid in a colander, rinse under cold water, and drain. Cut into rings about ¼-inch thick. Leave tentacles whole (if using).

Rinse cooked shrimp briefly and pat dry. Rinse celery and remove any wilted parts and loose "threads." Cut stalks in half lengthwise, then slice thinly on the diagonal. Peel carrots, slice lengthwise, and then cut into short julienned strips. Rinse parsley, shake dry, and chop leaves finely.

Combine lemon juice, salt, pepper, and olive oil in a bowl and whisk vigorously until creamy. Add squid, shrimp, vegetables, and parsley, and refrigerate for 2 hours. Before placing the salad on the table, stir and adjust seasonings to taste (salt, pepper, lemon juice). Garnish each person's serving with a lemon wedge.

Tuscan Bread Salad (Panzanella)

Serves 4:
3 cups white bread, cut into small cubes (can be up to 3 days old)
1 mild white onion
1 clove garlic
½ pound tomatoes, firm and ripe
½ cucumber (about ½ pound)
1 yellow bell pepper
2 cups arugula leaves
½ cup parsley sprigs
2–3 tablespoons red wine vinegar
Salt (preferably kosher or sea)
Freshly ground black pepper
⅓ cup extra virgin olive oil
1 tablespoon capers, rinsed

Prep time: 25 minutes
(+ 1 hour marinating)
Per serving approx: 252 calories
3 g protein/19 g fat/19 g carbohydrates

Toast bread cubes lightly in a dry pan over medium heat until lightly golden.

Peel onion, quarter, and slice thinly. Peel garlic and chop finely. Rinse tomatoes, cucumber, and bell pepper. Cut stem out of bell pepper and pull out ribs and seeds; cut stem end from tomato; and trim end off cucumber half. Finely dice all vegetables.

Remove wilted leaves and thick stems from arugula. Rinse arugula and parsley, shake dry, and chop both finely. For dressing, thoroughly whisk together vinegar, salt, pepper, and oil.

Combine toasted bread cubes, tomatoes, cucumbers, bell peppers, arugula, parsley, and dressing; let stand 5–10 minutes before serving. Add salt and pepper to taste—stir up panzanella once more, sprinkle with capers, and serve.

Minestrone Soup

Serves 4:
1 pound mixed vegetables (e.g., celery, zucchini, carrots, young savoy cabbage, spinach)
4 tomatoes
1 onion
2 cloves garlic
3 tablespoons olive oil
6 cups vegetable or meat stock
1 (14-ounce) can cooked white beans (e.g., cannellini, navy, great northern)
2 cups dried pasta (short type)
Salt (preferably kosher or sea)
Freshly ground black pepper
4 tablespoons freshly grated Parmesan or Pecorino

Prep time: 45 minutes
Per serving approx: 594 calories
35 g protein/13 g fat/85 g carbohydrates

Rinse all vegetables. Peel carrots. Dice tomatoes plus these types of vegetables: celery, zucchini, carrots. Cut these types into short strips: savoy cabbage, spinach. Peel onion and chop. Peel garlic and mince.

In a large pot, heat 1 tablespoon of the oil. Sauté onion and garlic for a minute or so. Add vegetable stock and vegetables; heat to a low boil.

Then, simmer the vegetables for about 15 minutes over medium-low heat with the lid halfway off.

Rinse beans in a colander under cold water, discarding liquid. Add beans and dry pasta to soup; simmer for 10 minutes or until the pasta is al dente.

Adjust salt and pepper to taste. Ladle soup into wide bowls, drizzle with remaining oil, and sprinkle with Parmesan. Serve with warm Italian bread and pesto, if desired.

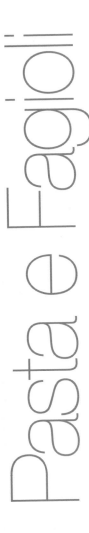

Pasta e Fagioli

Serves 4:
4 ounces pancetta or streaky smoked bacon
1 onion
2 tablespoons olive oil
2 (14-ounce) cans white beans (e.g., cannellini, great northern, navy)
1 quart vegetable or meat stock
1 (14-ounce) can whole peeled tomatoes (or 2 tomatoes)
2 cups dried short pasta (e.g., penne, orecchiette, fusilli)
¾ cup parsley sprigs
Salt (preferably kosher or sea)
Freshly ground black pepper

Prep time: 45 minutes
Per serving approx: 602 calories
32 g protein/10 g fat/93 g carbohydrates

Chop pancetta. Peel onion and chop. In a large pot, sauté pancetta and onion in 1 tablespoon of the oil, stirring. Continue until the fat on the bacon is translucent; add beans and stock. Bring to a low boil

Drain tomatoes and chop (omit juice). Or rinse fresh tomatoes and chop very finely. Stir into the soup. Purée two ladles of soup with a blender or hand blender. Return purée to the pot. Add pasta and continue simmering until it is al dente.

Meanwhile, rinse parsley and shake dry. Chop leaves very finely. Season soup to taste with salt and pepper. Sprinkle with parsley and drizzle with remaining oil. Serve at the table from the pot. Goes great with toasted, crusty Italian bread.

Serves 4: (entrée) or 8 (side dish)
2 pounds medium-sized eggplant
Salt (preferably kosher or sea)
3 balls fresh mozzarella (about 14 ounces)
¾ cup fresh basil leaves
2 (14-ounce) cans whole peeled tomatoes
Freshly ground black pepper
½ cup flour
⅔ cup olive oil
2 ounces freshly grated Parmesan

Prep time: 1¼ hours
Per serving approx: 746 calories (entrée)
33 g protein/54 g fat/35 g carbohydrates

Rinse eggplant and trim ends. Cut into lengthwise slices, about ½-inch thick. Sprinkle each with salt; let stand 15 minutes.

Drain the fresh mozzarella balls and slice thinly. Chop basil. Chop tomatoes and put in a large bowl with a little of the juice from the can, plus the basil, salt, and pepper.

Next, pat dry the eggplant slices. Spread flour on a plate. Season eggplant with pepper and dredge with flour on both sides to lightly coat.

Preheat oven to 350°F. In a pan, heat 2 tablespoons of the oil. Using medium heat, sauté one-fourth of the eggplant until brown on both sides. Remove and drain on paper towels. Add more oil and another batch of eggplant to the pan; continue in this way.

Line a large, greased baking dish with a layer of eggplant; spread with tomato mixture and top with fresh mozzarella slices. Add another layer of sautéed eggplant, etc., until all ingredients are used. Sprinkle with Parmesan and drizzle with any remaining oil. Bake on the middle rack for 30 minutes or until golden. Let rest 10 minutes; then cut and serve.

Roasted Fennel

Serves 4:
2 fennel bulbs (about 1½ pounds)
Salt (preferably kosher or sea)
2 tomatoes
¼ cup bread crumbs
¼ cup freshly grated Parmesan
Freshly ground black pepper
2 tablespoons butter

Prep time: 45 mintues
Per serving approx: 151 calories
5 g protein/8 g fat/17 g carbohydrates

Remove wilted stalks/leaves from fennel and cut off thick green stems. Save the nice green fronds and set aside. Cut both bulbs into four quarters, lengthwise. Cut out core and remove outer portion of bulb, if tough. In a pot, bring to a boil about 2 inches of salted water. Add fennel wedges, cover, and boil for 5 minutes.

Meanwhile, rinse tomatoes and dice very finely. Chop fennel fronds very finely. Drain cooked fennel in a colander and rinse under cold water. Pat dry.

Preheat oven to 375°F. In a greased baking dish, lay the fennel quarters side by side. Top with tomatoes and season lightly with salt. Combine bread crumbs with Parmesan, pepper, and fennel fronds, and sprinkle mixture over the top. Cut butter into bits and lay on top.

Bake fennel on the middle rack for about 20 minutes or until the bread crumb mixture is golden.

Serves 4:
4 large or 8 medium tomatoes
1 onion
2 cloves garlic
1 (3¾-ounce) can oil-packed sardines (don't confuse with anchovies)
½ cup fresh parsley sprigs
2 tablespoons pitted black olives (preferably kalamata or Niçoise)
¼ cup olive oil
¼ cup bread crumbs
¼ cup freshly grated Parmesan
1 tablespoon fresh lemon juice
1 teaspoon lemon zest
Salt (preferably kosher or sea)
Freshly ground black pepper

Prep time: 50 minutes
Per serving approx: 250 calories
6 g protein/18 g fat/18 g carbohydrates

Rinse tomatoes and cut off tops—scoop out contents (reserve). Discard seeds and chop tops and rest of tomato contents finely. Drain outer shell of tomatoes upside down on paper towels.

Peel onion and garlic; mince both. Drain sardines and chop. Chop parsley finely. Chop pitted olives finely.

Preheat oven to 350°F. In a pan, heat 1 tablespoon of the oil. Add and sauté onion and garlic. Stir in chopped tomato and parsley and cook uncovered over medium heat for about 5 minutes.

Stir in olives and sardines. Remove pan from heat and let cool slightly, then add bread crumbs, Parmesan, lemon juice, and lemon zest. Season with salt and pepper. Stuff the tomato shells by filling generously with the tomato-Parmesan-bread crumb mixture (overflowing OK). Arrange tomatoes side by side in a greased baking dish; sprinkle with remaining oil.

Bake tomatoes on the middle rack for about 30 minutes or until golden on top.

Caponata

Serves 4:
2 stalks celery
1 onion
2 cloves garlic
1 eggplant (about ¾ pound)
2 medium tomatoes (or 1 large, about ½ pound)
6 tablespoons olive oil
Salt (preferably kosher or sea)
Freshly ground black pepper
1 tablespoon pitted imported green olives
½ cup fresh basil sprigs
2 tablespoons red wine vinegar
½ tablespoon sugar
1–2 tablespoons capers
1 tablespoon pine nuts

Prep time: 45 minutes
Per serving approx: 247 calories
2 g protein/22 g fat/13 g carbohydrates

Rinse celery, trim off ends of stalks, and slice rest thinly. Peel onion and garlic. Cut onion in half and then into thin strips. Mince garlic. Rinse eggplant, cut crosswise into thin slices, then cut slices into fourths or eighths (bite-size pieces). Rinse tomatoes and dice finely.

In a large pan, heat half the oil. Stir in at least half the eggplant and brown well over medium heat. Remove, then add another 2 tablespoons of the oil to the pan; brown the rest of the eggplant. Remove.

In the pan, combine remaining oil, onion, and garlic. Sauté briefly. Stir in all the eggplant, celery, and tomatoes; season with salt and pepper. Cover and simmer over medium heat for about 5 minutes.

In the meantime, chop olives; pull off basil leaves (brush off leaves if necessary) and leave whole.

Add basil, olives, vinegar, sugar, and capers to eggplant and cook, uncovered, for about 15 more minutes or until the vegetables are almost creamy, stirring occasionally.

Toast pine nuts in a small dry pan, stirring constantly, until golden. Let caponata cool and sprinkle with pine nuts.

Rosemary Potatoes

Serves 4:
1¼ pounds potatoes (firm type: red, fingerling, or Yukon gold)
1 sprig rosemary
3–4 tablespoons olive oil
Salt (preferably kosher or sea)

Prep time: 50 minutes
Per serving approx: 234 calories
3 g protein/14 g fat/26 g carbohydrates

Scrub potatoes under running water. Then boil, for 20–30 minutes depending on size, until tender but not mushy. Drain and let cool.

Slip peels off of cooled potatoes and quarter potatoes lengthwise. Rinse rosemary, shake dry, and strip off needles. Chop needles if desired.

In a large frying pan, heat oil. Add potatoes, preferably side by side. Brown over medium heat and turn. Add rosemary, season with salt and pepper to taste, and brown as much as possible on each side. Serve.

Pasta

Perhaps pasta is what we most often associate with Italian cooking. But did you know that noodles are not indigenous to Italy? No one's sure where pasta originated, but we do know that both Greece and the Arab world had their influences. By the early 1900s, though, pasta had firmly taken hold in households Italy-wide. The Italians went on not only to perfect but also to popularize its many pasta dishes thoughout the world. In Italy, pasta is served as a primo, or first course, before the meat and vegetable courses.

For all of the following recipes, cooking pasta to the "al dente" stage is very important. The noodles should still have a bite to them, not be mushy, but also not taste starchy—rather, nicely chewy. For a pound of pasta, begin with three or more quarts of water and bring it to an aggressive boil—then add a couple teaspoons of table salt, and then the dry pasta. No need to add olive oil to the boiling water, nor to the cooked pasta later. Stir briefly, return the pot to a boil, then reduce heat so that it maintains a gentle, rolling boil. Each type of pasta takes a different amount of time; consult the package directions for specifics. But there's no harm in beginning to test a piece around the eight-minute mark. When al dente, drain and toss immediately with whichever sauce you've chosen, and enjoy.

Basic Italian Tomato Sauce with Pasta

Serves 4:
1¼ pounds ripe, bright-red tomatoes
1 small carrot
1 stalk celery
1 onion
2 cloves garlic
1 teaspoon fresh rosemary needles
3 tablespoons olive oil
Salt (preferably kosher or sea)
Freshly ground black pepper
½ cup fresh basil leaves
Table salt for pasta water
1 pound pasta

Prep time: 45 minutes
Per serving approx: 561 calories
16 g protein/12 g fat/96 g carbohydrates

Remove cores from tomatoes. Place tomatoes in a bowl, pour boiling water over the top, and wait until the peels loosen, about a minute. Place tomatoes in a colander and rinse under cold water. Slip off peels; remove seeds with your fingers. Dice tomatoes.

Peel and rinse carrot, rinse celery, and dice both finely. Peel onion and garlic; mince both. Chop rosemary.

Heat oil in a pot. Briefly sauté onion and garlic. Add carrot and celery; sauté briefly. Add tomatoes and rosemary, season with salt and pepper to taste, and simmer over medium heat for 20–25 minutes, stirring occasionally. Add water if sauce becomes too thick. Before serving, add fresh basil leaves (cut into strips) and salt to taste.

Boil 4–5 quarts water in a large pot; then add salt. Add pasta, stir occasionally, and cook until al dente.

Drain pasta in a colander, immediately mix with sauce, and transfer to wide-rimmed shallow bowls. Let guests freshly grate a chunk of good Parmesan at the table, to top the dish.

Pesto Pasta

Serves 8:
2 cups basil leaves (or one large bunch)
2 cloves garlic
²⁄₃ cup pine nuts
¹⁄₃ cup plus 1 tablespoon extra virgin olive oil
2 ounces freshly grated Parmesan
Salt (preferably kosher or sea)
Freshly ground black pepper
Table salt for pasta water
2 pounds pasta (for 8 people)

Prep time: 20 minutes
Per serving approx: 601 calories
20 g protein/19 g fat/87 g carbohydrates

Wipe off basil leaves and remove from stems. Peel garlic.

Combine basil, garlic, and pine nuts and purée at medium speed (use blender or food processor) while gradually adding oil. Stir in Parmesan, salt, and pepper—ready!

Meanwhile, boil pasta until al dente in salted water. Stir together 1 tablespoon pesto and 1 tablespoon hot pasta water for each serving (add more pesto as desired); mix with drained pasta and serve.

If covered with a layer of oil and tightly sealed, pesto keeps for about a week in the refrigerator.

Spaghetti Carbonara

Serves 4:
Table salt for pasta water
1 pound spaghetti
4 ounces pancetta or bacon
1 clove garlic
1 tablespoon olive oil
2 very fresh eggs
$\frac{1}{3}$ cup heavy cream
2 ounces freshly grated Parmesan or pecorino (or mixture)
Salt (preferably kosher or sea)
Freshly ground black pepper

Prep time: 20 minutes
Per serving approx: 653 calories
32 g protein/19 g fat/87 g carbohydrates

In a large pot, boil 4–5 quarts water; then add salt. Push spaghetti down into it with a mixing spoon until all the pasta is under water. Cook until al dente—usually about 8–10 minutes, but it's best to test it earlier. Place a large bowl and four spaghetti plates in a warm oven (about 170°F).

Meanwhile, finely dice pancetta or bacon. Peel garlic and mince. Heat oil in a medium-sized pan; cook diced pancetta until slightly crispy, stirring occasionally.

In the warmed bowl, combine eggs, cream, and Parmesan—whisk together. Drain pasta and immediately add to the egg-cream mixture along with the hot bacon. Add salt and pepper to taste, mix well, and transfer immediately to warmed plates to serve.

Pancetta Pasta (Amatriciana)

Serves 4:
1 mild white onion
4 ounces pancetta or smoked bacon
2–3 dried red chiles or 1 teaspoon crushed red pepper flakes
3 medium tomatoes
2 tablespoons olive oil
⅓ cup dry white wine
Table salt for pasta water
1 pound "long" pasta (e.g., bucatini, spaghetti, perciatelli, or any narrow ribbon pasta)
Salt (preferably kosher or sea)

Prep time: 30 minutes
Per serving approx: 579 calories
23 g protein/11 g fat/92 g carbohydrates

Peel onion and chop finely. Chop bacon. Crush red chile in a mortar or chop but be careful! Wear gloves and wash hands well; don't touch your eyes. Or use flakes instead. Remove tomato cores and discard; pour boiling water over the tomatoes. Rinse under cold water, slip off peels, and dice tomatoes.

Bring water to a boil for pasta; then add salt. Heat oil in a large pan. Add bacon and cook over medium heat, stirring. Add onion and chiles; briefly sauté. Pour in wine and stir in tomatoes; reduce heat to low. Cover and simmer sauce for about 5–10 minutes.

To the boiling water, add pasta, stir occasionally, and cook until al dente. Season the sauce to taste with kosher or sea salt. Drain pasta, mix well with the sauce in the pan, and serve immediately.

Lemon-Cream Spaghetti

Serves 4:
Table salt for pasta
1 pound spaghetti
2 cloves garlic
1 lemon
1 tablespoon butter
1⅓ cups tender, shelled peas
8 ounces heavy cream
Salt (preferably kosher or sea)
Freshly ground black pepper

Prep time: 30 minutes
Per serving approx: 629 calories
19 g protein/19 g fat/96 g carbohydrates

Bring to a boil 4 quarts water; then add salt. Add pasta, press under the water, and cook until al dente.

Meanwhile, peel garlic and slice thinly. Rinse lemon and pat dry. Remove zest, carefully avoiding the bitter white part of the rind. Cut lemon in half and squeeze out juice.

Melt butter in a pot. Briefly sauté garlic and peas. Add cream and lemon zest and simmer over medium heat until slightly reduced. Stir in 2 tablespoons of the fresh lemon juice. Salt and pepper to taste. Remove from heat.

Drain pasta in a colander; pour into the pot with the lemon cream and mix briefly, transfer to wide pasta bowls, and enjoy.

Gorgonzola Pasta

Serves 4:
8 ounces gorgonzola
1 small onion
2 cloves garlic
1 tablespoon olive oil
1 tablespoon butter
1¾ cups heavy cream
1 pound pasta (e.g., tagliatelle, spaghetti, or penne)
Salt (preferably kosher or sea)
Freshly ground black pepper

Prep time: 30 minutes
Per serving approx: 946 calories
30 g protein/52 g fat/93 g carbohydrates

Cut gorgonzola cheese into small cubes. Peel onion and garlic; chop both finely.

In a pot, heat oil and butter until butter melts. Stir in onion and garlic; sauté briefly. Turn heat to very low and add gorgonzola cubes and cream. Heat sauce and continue stirring until gorgonzola melts and the sauce is slightly thickened.

Meanwhile, boil 4–5 quarts water; then add salt. Add pasta, stir occasionally, and cook until al dente. Drain in a colander.

Season sauce to taste with pepper and, carefully, with salt if desired (the gorgonzola is already salty); mix with the hot pasta and transfer to wide pasta bowls for serving.

Serves 4:
1 small eggplant (about 1/3 pound)
1 zucchini
1 yellow bell pepper
1 onion
2 cloves garlic
3 tablespoons olive oil
1 (14-ounce) can whole peeled tomatoes
Salt (preferably kosher or sea)
Freshly ground black pepper
Table salt for pasta water
1 pound penne or fusilli
1/2 cup basil leaves
1 ball fresh mozzarella (about 5 ounces)

Prep time: 40 minutes
Per serving approx: 650 calories
27 g protein/17 g fat/97 g carbohydrates

Rinse eggplant, zucchini, and bell pepper. Trim ends off all, and remove stem, ribs and seeds from pepper. Cut each into 1/2-inch cubes. Peel onion and garlic; chop both finely.

Heat oil. Briefly sauté onion, garlic, and other vegetables. Chop tomatoes and add along with their juice to pan. Season with salt and pepper. Cover and simmer on medium-low for about 20 minutes, stirring occasionally.

In the meantime, bring to a boil 4–5 quarts water; then add salt. Pour in pasta, stir, and cook until al dente.

Cut basil leaves into strips, dice fresh mozzarella, and add both to the vegetable sauce. If desired, replace cover to let cheese melt slightly.

Drain pasta, mix with sauce, and serve immediately.

Spaghetti with Clams (Vongole)

Serves 4:
2½ pounds clams
Table salt for pasta water
1 pound spaghetti
2 cloves garlic
1 large tomato (about ½ pound)
¼ cup olive oil
1 cup parsley sprigs
Freshly ground black pepper
Salt (preferably kosher or sea)
1 dried red chile or ½ teaspoon crushed red pepper flakes (optional)

Prep time: 30 minutes
Approx per serving: 769
52 g protein/28 g fat/96 g carbohydrates

Place clams in a colander and rinse well. Clams close their shells if they're fresh. At this point, throw away any that don't close.

Bring to a boil 4–5 quarts water; then add 2 teaspoons table salt. Pour in pasta, push under water with a wooden spoon, and cook until al dente.

Meanwhile, continue preparing the sauce. Peel garlic, slice, and then cut into thin strips. Rinse tomato and dice finely.

In a wide pot or pan, heat 2 tablespoons of the oil. Add wet clams and garlic, cover, and cook over high heat for 5 minutes. Now the shells should open. Make absolutely sure you throw away any clams that are still closed. Reserve pan liquid.

Leave a few clams in the shells for garnish. Pull the others out of the shells with a fork or tweezers (if desired). Pour the cooking liquid through a paper coffee filter to remove any sand from the clam shells. Rinse parsley, shake dry, and chop leaves finely.

Heat remaining 2 tablespoons oil in a pot. Stir in tomatoes and heat. Add clams (if removed from shells), strained cooking liquid, parsley, salt (to taste), pepper, and dried red chile (or use flakes) and simmer uncovered for about 3 minutes over low heat. Remove chile (unless flakes).

Drain al dente pasta in a colander. Then mix well with sauce in the pot. Transfer to pre-warmed plates. Place clams in shells on top. Ready to eat!

Spaghetti Puttanesca

Serves 4:
6–8 anchovy fillets in oil
2 cloves garlic
1 fresh red Fresno chile
Table salt for pasta water
1 pound spaghetti
¼ cup olive oil
1 (14-ounce) can whole peeled tomatoes
6 tablespoons dry red wine
2 tablespoons capers
2 tablespoons pitted black olives (kalamata or Niçoise preferred)
Salt (preferably kosher or sea)

Prep time: 30 minutes
Per serving approx: 620 calories
18 g protein/18 g fat/92 g carbohydrates

Drain anchovies well and chop finely. Peel garlic and mince. Rinse chile, trim off stem, and then decide: If you like spicy food, finely chop the pepper with the seeds. If not, remove seeds and ribs. When working with hot peppers, wear gloves, and don't touch your face.

In a large pot, bring to a boil 4–5 quarts water; then add 2 teaspoons table salt. Add pasta and press down with a wooden spoon until immersed; cook until al dente.

Meanwhile, continue preparing the sauce. Heat oil in a pot. Stir in anchovies, garlic, and chile; sauté briefly. Chop tomatoes and add with the wine to the pot. Simmer, uncovered, over medium heat for 10 minutes.

Drain and rinse capers. Cut pitted olives into strips. Add both to the sauce, mix, and taste. Next, season to taste with salt (if needed). Drain pasta, mix with sauce, and serve immediately.

Broccoli Orecchiette

Serves 4:

Table salt for pasta water
1 pound orecchiette
1 pound broccoli
4–8 anchovy fillets in oil
2–4 cloves garlic
1–2 dried red chiles or crushed red pepper flakes to taste
¼ cup extra virgin olive oil

Prep time: 20 minutes
Per serving approx: 593 calories
20 g protein/16 g fat/92 g carbohydrates

Bring to a boil at least 5 quarts water; then add 2 teaspoons salt. Add pasta, stir, and cook until al dente. Orecchiette always take a little longer than other pasta—about 10–12 minutes—but test one prior to that.

Meanwhile, prepare the vegetables: Rinse broccoli and cut off florets. Peel stems and slice (about ¼-inch-thick). Cut large slices in half. After about 8 minutes, add broccoli to pasta in the boiling water; cook together.

Drain anchovy fillets and chop finely. Peel garlic and slice, then cut into thin strips. Crush dried red chile in a mortar or crumble with hands (wear gloves and don't touch your face). Or use flakes instead.

Drain broccoli and pasta in a colander. Heat oil, anchovies, garlic, and crushed chile in the pot briefly. Stir in pasta and broccoli; mix well. Adjust salt to taste and serve.

Lasagna with Two Sauces

Serves 6–8:
For the tomato sauce:
1 carrot
1 stalk celery
2 ounces pancetta
1 onion
2 cloves garlic
1 tablespoon butter
2 tablespoons olive oil
10–12 ounces ground meat
1 (14-ounce) can whole peeled tomatoes
1¼ cups beef broth
Salt (preferably kosher or sea)
Freshly ground black pepper

Prep time: 1¼ hours
Per serving (8) approx:
579 calories
31 g protein/35 g fat/
35 g carbohydrate

For the cream sauce:
¼ cup butter
Scant ½ cup flour
3 cups plus 1 tablespoon milk
Salt (preferably kosher or sea)
Freshly ground black pepper
Freshly grated nutmeg
For layering:
8 ounces lasagna sheets
Table salt for pasta water
2 balls fresh mozzarella
(about ½ pound)
4 ounces freshly grated Parmesan
1 tablespoon butter

FOR TOMATO SAUCE: peel carrot, rinse celery, and dice both. Chop pancetta. Peel onion and garlic; chop both.

Heat butter and oil in a large pan. Stir in pancetta, carrot, celery, onion, and garlic; sauté briefly. Add ground meat, sautéing until crumbly.

Chop tomatoes and add to pan along with their juice and the beef broth. Simmer, covered, for 1 hour. Salt and pepper to taste.

FOR CREAM SAUCE: melt butter in a pot but don't brown. Add flour while stirring with a wooden spoon until smooth. Gradually add milk, while whisking, until smooth. Simmer for 5–10 minutes until thickened. Season to taste with salt, pepper, and nutmeg.

Boil 5 quarts water; then add salt. Cook lasagna pasta for 4–5 minutes until sheets are bendable and almost al dente; drain and rinse with cold water.

Dice fresh mozzarella. Preheat oven to 375°F. Grease a large rectangular or oval baking dish. Pour in some of the cream sauce. Arrange pasta sheets on top, then tomato sauce, more cream sauce, fresh mozzarella, and more pasta. Continue layering in this manner. Top with remaining cream sauce; sprinkle with Parmesan and bits of butter. Bake for 40 minutes.

Quick Salmon Lasagna

Serves 4:
2 cups frozen peas
Table salt for pasta water
16 dried lasagna pasta sheets
10–12 ounces salmon fillets
1 cup ricotta (about 8 ounces)
½ cup heavy cream
From ½ lemon: 1 tablespoon juice and grated zest
Salt (preferably kosher or sea)
Freshly ground black pepper
¾ cup basil sprigs
2 tablespoons pine nuts
2 tablespoons freshly grated Parmesan or pecorino
2–3 tablespoons olive oil

Prep time: 40 minutes
Per serving approx: 857 calories
37 g protein/18 g fat/134 g carbohydrates

Break apart peas and thaw.

Boil 4–5 quarts water; then add salt. Add pasta sheets and cook until al dente. Drain pasta and rinse under cold water. Lay sheets side by side on a damp, non-terry dish towel.

Check salmon for bones, and remove any you find with tweezers. Cut salmon into narrow strips.

In a bowl, stir together ricotta, cream, lemon juice, and lemon zest. Add a little salt and pepper. Rinse basil, shake dry, and remove leaves (discard stems).

Preheat oven to 425°F. Grease four small oven-proof dishes (or one large shallow one).

In each small dish, place 1 pasta sheet, a portion salmon, peas, and basil leaves; spread with ricotta. Top with another pasta sheet and repeat layers, using 4 pasta sheets total per dish. If using a large baking dish, layer 4 servings side by side.

Combine pine nuts and Parmesan—top lasagna with this mixture. Drizzle with oil. Bake lasagna on middle rack for about 10 minutes, until top is golden and salmon is cooked through. Serve.

Risotto, Pizza, and Polenta

During an Italian lunch, or main meal, the risotto, pizza, or polenta would form the *primo*, or first course—as does pasta. These carbohydrates provide a feeling of fullness and continue to keep energy levels high throughout the rest of the day. Then, in the evening, a slice of pizza purchased from a street vendor is often consumed as the evening meal. In Italy, dinners are more like "snacks" and are eaten quite late at night.

In the United States, we have the flexibility to enjoy these Italian dishes just about any time we want to. On many occasions, they're not just a course, but a one-dish meal to themselves.

Saffron Risotto

Serves 4:
1 small onion
4 cups beef stock
3$\frac{1}{2}$ tablespoons butter
A scant 2 cups arborio rice (do not rinse)
$\frac{1}{3}$ cup dry white wine
A few threads saffron
2 ounces freshly grated Parmesan
Salt (preferably kosher or sea)
Freshly ground black pepper

Prep time: 40 minutes
Per serving approx: 533 calories
14 g protein/15 g fat/77 g carbohydrates

Peel and chop onion. Heat stock. Set aside half the butter. Melt rest in a medium to large pot.

Add onions and sauté briefly. Then add rice and stir briefly. Using high heat, pour in the wine. When the wine has evaporated, change to medium heat.

Add a ladle of hot stock and cook, stirring, until the liquid has evaporated. Add the next ladle full, and keep stirring. Repeat the process.

When you're down to the last ladle of stock, add the saffron into it (crumble threads with your fingers) and stir—then add that mixture into the risotto.

If the risotto is creamy and smooth, and the grains of rice are tender yet firm, it's done.

Fold remaining butter and grated Parmesan into the risotto and taste. Adjust salt and pepper, and serve.

Porcini Risotto

Serves 4:
1 1/2 ounces dried porcini mushrooms
1 small onion
1 small carrot
1 stalk celery
1/2 cup parsley sprigs
2 tablespoons olive oil
A scant 2 cups arborio rice
2 canned whole peeled tomatoes
1 tablespoon butter
2 ounces freshly grated Parmesan
Salt (preferably sea or kosher)
Freshly ground black pepper

Prep time: 1 hour
Per serving approx: 548 calories
15 g protein/14 g fat/89 g carbohydrates

Put dried porcinis in a small bowl, cover with 1 quart lukewarm water, and soak for 30 minutes, until soft.

Meanwhile, peel onion and carrot. Rinse celery and parsley. Finely chop these 4 ingredients and mix together.

Remove porcinis from liquid, rinse, and chop finely (reserve liquid). Pour porcini-soaking liquid through a paper coffee filter to remove any grit. Almost exactly 3 cups should remain—heat to a gentle boil. Dice tomatoes.

Heat oil in a pot and briefly sauté vegetable mixture and porcinis. Stir in rice, then tomatoes.

While stirring, gradually add the hot porcini liquid one ladle full at a time to the rice. Only add the next ladle when the previous one is incorporated. Add water or stock if extra liquid is needed. Finally, fold in butter and Parmesan; adjust salt and pepper to taste.

Asparagus-Lemon Risotto

Serves 4:
1 pound green asparagus spears
1 small onion
2 cloves garlic
3¼ cups chicken stock
½ to 1 lemon
3½ ounces fontina cheese
3 tablespoons butter
A scant 2 cups arborio rice
1 cup dry white wine
A few sprigs basil
Salt (preferably kosher or sea)
Freshly ground black pepper

Prep time: 1 hour
Per serving approx: 594 calories
16 g protein/17 g fat/82 g carbohydrates

Rinse asparagus and trim off tough ends. Cut off the tips as well (about 1 inch) and reserve for later. Cut the rest into ½-inch pieces. Peel onion and garlic; chop both finely. Heat stock to a gentle boil.

Rinse lemon, pat dry, and grate off a thin layer of zest (avoid getting any white "pith," which imparts a bitter taste). Lemon zest should be in fine strips: if not, chop. Dice fontina cheese.

In another pot, melt half the butter and briefly sauté onion, garlic, and asparagus pieces (but not tips) while stirring. Add rice and stir until grains are shiny.

Add wine and let evaporate over high heat while stirring. Then add 1 ladle hot stock and switch risotto pot to medium heat. Keep stirring diligently while gradually adding stock one ladle at a time. Let liquid incorporate each time before adding the next. After 10 minutes, add the asparagus tips and after another 10 minutes, do a taste test. When risotto is creamy and grains are firm yet tender (easy to chew), it's ready for the next step.

Remove basil leaves from stems and cut into narrow strips. Add fontina cheese, lemon zest, basil strips, and remaining butter to the pot and fold in until the cheese has melted in the hot rice mixture. Salt and pepper to taste, and serve.

Serves 4:
1 leek
2 cloves garlic
2 cups arugula leaves
1 quart beef stock
1 tomato
4 ounces prosciutto
3 tablespoons butter
A scant 2 cups arborio rice
2 ounces freshly grated pecorino cheese (or Parmesan)
1 tablespoon mascarpone or crème fraîche (optional)
Salt (preferably kosher or sea)
Nutmeg

Prep time: 1 hour
Per serving approx: 571 calories
22 g protein/16 g fat/17 g carbohydrates

Remove roots and dark-green, wilted parts from leek. Slit open lengthwise and bend apart individual leaves, rinsing very well under cold running water to remove grit. Cut leek into fine strips crosswise. Peel garlic and mince. Remove wilted leaves from arugula and trim thick stems. Rinse and pat dry arugula leaves—reserve some for garnish and finely chop the rest. Heat stock to a gentle boil. Rinse tomato and dice finely. Cut prosciutto into short strips.

In a separate large pot, melt half the butter. Briefly sauté leek and garlic. Add rice and chopped arugula.

Now it follows the traditional risotto technique: add a ladle of stock and stir diligently. Each time, when the stock has evaporated, add some more—and so on.

When you notice the rice is almost al dente, coarsely tear or chop remaining arugula.

Stir in tomato, prosciutto, pecorino, remaining butter, and, if desired, mascarpone. Season risotto to taste with salt and nutmeg; top with remaining arugula, and enjoy.

Homemade Gnocchi

Serves 4:
2¼ pounds potatoes (russet or similar variety)
1 cup flour, plus more for coating
½ cup durum semolina
2 teaspoons kosher salt

Prep time: 45 minutes (+ 1 hour resting time)
Per serving approx: 391 calories
11 g protein/1 g fat/85 g carbohydrates

Scrub potatoes and cover halfway with cold water in a large pot. Bring water to a boil, cover, and cook over medium heat until tender (20 to 35 minutes).

Drain potatoes and let cool slightly, but peel while still warm. Press through a potato ricer. If you don't have a ricer, mash with a fork or potato masher. But don't purée, or the potatoes will turn to paste.

To mashed potaotes (make sure they're not too hot), add flour, semolina, and the salt. Knead all this together with your hands and form sections of it into long rolls the thickness of an index finger. Cut the rolls into 1-inch pieces. Roll each piece in flour, then gently press down on one side of each with tines of a fork so each gnocchi has ridges. **TIP:** Spread the gnocchi out on non-terry dish towels and let rest 1 hour or even longer.

In a large pot, heat a generous amount of salted water. When it starts boiling, drop in the gnocchi. When the gnocchi rise to the top, turn the heat to medium. Let cook for about 2–3 minutes. Take care not to let them become too soft nor soggy. Test one for doneness.

Remove gnocchi with a slotted spoon and transfer to plates. Toss gently with sauce immediately: try melted butter and Parmesan; or serve with basic tomato sauce on page 34, or pesto (page 36).

Roasted Polenta with Meat and Vegetables

Serves 4:
Salt (preferably kosher or sea)
1²/₃ cups dried polenta
1 large onion
2 cloves garlic
2 carrots
2 stalks celery
4 ounces Italian salami
¼ cup olive oil
1 pound ground meat
1 (14-ounce) can whole peeled tomatoes
½ cup dry red wine
½ teaspoon crushed red pepper flakes
1 teaspoon dried thyme
4 ounces freshly grated Parmesan

Prep time: 1½ hours
Per serving approx: 932 calories
43 g protein/52 g fat/65 g carbohydrates

In a large pot, boil 4 cups water; then add 1 teaspoon table salt. Pour in polenta and stir to mix well. Cook, covered, on low heat for 10 minutes.

Pour polenta onto a large, lined baking sheet or cutting board. Spread out to a thickness of about ¾ inch. Allow to cool and solidify.

Peel onion and garlic; chop both finely. Peel carrots. Rinse celery and trim ends. Pull off any loose "threads." Chop carrots, celery, and salami very finely.

In a pan, heat 2 tablespoons of the oil. Briefly sauté onion and garlic. Stir in vegetables and salami and sauté briefly. Add and brown ground meat until cooked through and crumbly. Chop tomatoes and add to pan along with their juice, red wine, and crushed red pepper flakes.

Add thyme and stir; simmer uncovered on medium for 15 minutes. Salt and pepper to taste.

Preheat oven to 375°F. Brush a narrow rectangular baking dish with a thin layer of the remaining oil.

Cut polenta into strips no more than 1-inch wide. Rinse knife periodically.

Fill baking dish with alternating layers of polenta slices and ground meat mixture. Top with Parmesan and drizzle with oil.

Bake polenta on the middle rack for 35 minutes, and until top is golden.

Makes 2 round pizzas:
2 cups flour, plus flour for shaping
Salt (preferably kosher or sea)
¼ cup olive oil
1 packet yeast

Prep time: 1 hour
Per serving (8) approx: 176 calories
4 g protein/7 g fat/24 g carbohydrates

Pour flour into a bowl with 1 large pinch of salt and the oil. Separately, stir yeast into 2/3 cup lukewarm water until smooth.

Mix flour, oil, salt, and yeast-water together briefly—add a little flour if dough is too sticky. Then pour a little flour onto a work surface, put the dough on it, and knead vigorously until pliable (or use the dough hooks on an electric mixer).

Grease a bowl and put the ball of dough in it; cover with a cloth. After 30–45 minutes the dough will have doubled in size and is ready to be punched down, formed, topped, and baked.

Pizza Margherita

Serves 4:
½ recipe basic pizza dough (page 72)
1 onion
2 cloves garlic
2 tablespoons olive oil, plus oil for pan
2 (14-ounce) cans whole peeled tomatoes
Salt (preferably kosher or sea)
Freshly ground black pepper
3 balls fresh mozzarella (about 14 ounces)
¾ cup basil sprigs

Prep time: 1½ hours
Per serving approx: 566 calories
34 g protein/31 g fat/38 g carbohydrates

Prepare basic pizza dough. While it is rising, peel onion and garlic; chop both finely. In a pan heat 1 tablespoon of the oil and sauté onion and garlic. Chop tomatoes and add to pan with juice from the can. Simmer for 20 minutes uncovered on medium heat, stirring occasionally. Salt and pepper to taste.

Preheat oven to 425°F. Brush baking sheet with a little oil and roll out the dough directly onto it so that edges are bit thicker than the middle.

Spread tomato sauce onto dough. Slice fresh mozzarella. Pull off basil leaves (reserve some for garnish). Place mozzarella slices and basil leaves on top of tomato sauce; drizzle with remaining oil.

Bake pizza on middle oven rack for about 25 minutes. The cheese should be melted but not browned. Garnish with reserved basil; cut slices and serve.

Pepper-Artichoke Pizza

Serves 4:
½ recipe basic pizza dough (page 72)
2 (14-ounce) cans whole peeled tomatoes
2 cloves garlic
Salt (preferably kosher or sea)
Freshly ground black pepper
2 yellow bell peppers
1 cup marinated artichoke hearts
2 balls fresh mozzarella (about 8 ounces)
1 teaspoon dried oregano or thyme
2 tablespoons olive oil, plus oil for the pan

Prep time: 1½ hours
Per serving approx: 471 calories
24 g protein/24 g fat/43 g carbohydrates

Prepare dough, let rise, and roll out onto a greased baking sheet.

Drain tomatoes and squeeze juice out gently; discard juice. Chop tomatoes very finely or purée briefly with a hand blender. Peel garlic, squeeze through a press, and add to tomatoes. Salt and pepper to taste; spread sauce onto dough.

Preheat oven to 425°F.

Rinse bell peppers and remove stem, ribs, and seeds; quarter peppers and then cut into strips. Quarter artichoke hearts. Dice fresh mozzarella.

Distribute vegetables over tomato sauce and sprinkle with salt, pepper, and oregano. Top with fresh mozzarella cubes and drizzle with olive oil. Bake pizza on middle rack for about 25 minutes until the cheese melts but is not browned. Remove, slice, and enjoy.

Serves 4:
$^1/_2$ recipe basic pizza dough (page 72)
About 1 pound cheeses (e.g., fresh mozzarella, gorgonzola, ricotta salata, and pecorino)
Several sprigs fresh thyme or sage
4–6 marinated pepperoncini
2 tablespoons olive oil, plus oil for baking sheet
Salt (preferably kosher or sea), optional

Prep time: 1$^1/_2$ hours
Per serving approx: 601 calories
29 g protein/42 g fat/28 g carbohydrates

Prepare pizza dough, let rise, and then roll out directly onto a lightly greased baking sheet so that edges are thicker than the middle.

Preheat oven to 475°F. Dice fresh mozzarella and gorgonzola; break up ricotta salata with a fork; grate pecorino. Mix all cheeses and scatter on top of the dough.

Rinse thyme or sage and shake dry. Strip thyme leaves from stems or cut sage into strips. Cut pepperoncini into rings.

Sprinkle herbs over the cheeses. Season very lightly with salt (optional). Place pepperoncini on top and drizzle with remaining oil. Bake pizza on the middle rack for 15 minutes and until golden.

Serves 4:
1/2 recipe basic pizza dough (page 72)
3/4 cup fresh parsley sprigs
2 cloves garlic
1/2 teaspoon crushed red pepper flakes
2 cups plus 2 tablespoons canned chopped tomatoes
Salt (preferably kosher or sea)
3 tablespoons oil, plus oil for baking sheet
1 1/3 pounds seafood (preferably pre-cooked; e.g., shrimp, mussels, clams, squid rings)
Freshly ground black pepper

Prep time: 1 1/2 hours
Per serving approx: 458 calories
36 g protein/20 g fat/32 g carbohydrates

Prepare pizza dough, let rise, and roll out onto greased baking sheet. Leave edges a bit thicker.

Preheat oven to 450°F. Rinse parsley, shake dry, and pull off leaves. Peel garlic. Chop parsley and garlic, and mix with chopped tomatoes along with the pepper flakes. Add a little salt and 1 tablespoon of the oil. Spread sauce onto dough.

Distribute cooked seafood on pizza, sprinkle with remaining oil, and grind black pepper over the top. Bake on middle rack for about 20 minutes—just until the crust is brown. The rest just needs to be heated through.

Prosciutto-Pecorino Pizza

Serves 4:
½ recipe basic pizza dough (page 72)
2 tablespoons olive oil, plus oil for baking sheet
1 pound green asparagus
5 green onions
Salt (preferably kosher or sea)
1 (14-ounce) can whole peeled tomatoes
Freshly ground black pepper
2 ounces freshly grated pecorino
4 ounces prosciutto di Parma, paper thin (or other prosciutto)

Prep time: 1½ hours
Per serving approx: 395 calories
20 g protein/21 g fat/33 g carbohydrates

Prepare pizza dough and let rise. Oil the baking sheet lightly and roll out dough onto it directly. Leave edges slightly thicker.

Rinse asparagus and trim ends. Cut spears into 2-inch pieces. Remove roots and dark-green parts from green onions; rinse and halve lengthwise.

Preheat oven to 425°F.

Bring a large amount of salted water to a boil. Boil asparagus and green onions for 2 minutes; rinse under cold water and drain.

Chop tomatoes and mix with a little of their juice, salt, and pepper. Spread onto the dough. Top with vegetables, sprinkle with grated pecorino, and drizzle with olive oil. Bake pizza on middle rack for about 20 minutes. Remove pizza from oven, top with prosciutto, slice, and enjoy.

Calzone

Serves 4:

For the dough:

1½ cups plus 2 tablespoons flour
Salt (preferably kosher or sea)
¼ cup olive oil, plus oil for baking sheet
1 packet yeast

For the filling:

2 ounces cooked ham
1 small, firm tomato
½ cup parsley sprigs
1 ball fresh mozzarella (4–5 ounces)
⅔ cup ricotta
1 egg
2 ounces freshly grated Parmesan or pecorino
1 clove garlic
Salt (preferably kosher or sea)
Freshly ground black pepper
2 tablespoons olive oil for brushing on

Prep time: 1¾ hours
Per serving approx: 661 calories
31 g protein/39 g fat/46 g carbohydrates

Combine flour, salt, and olive oil. Separately, stir yeast into ⅔ cup lukewarm water; combine with flour mixture. Transfer dough to a work surface; knead vigorously. Place dough in a greased bowl; cover and let rise 1 hour. The dough should approximately double in size.

Meanwhile, prepare the filling. Dice ham. Rinse tomato and dice finely. Rinse parsley, shake dry, and chop very finely.

Dice fresh mozzarella and mix with ricotta and egg. Stir in ham, tomato, parsley, and Parmesan. Peel garlic, squeeze through a press, and add. Season filling with salt and pepper.

Preheat oven to 425°F. Lightly flour work surface, and roll out dough thinly into a large round circle.

Place dough on greased baking sheet; let half hang over one edge. Distribute filling on the half that rests on the pan, but leave space near outside edges. Fold the overhanging side over the filling and carefully press the edges together and pinch closed to seal. Brush with olive oil.

Bake on the middle rack for about 25 minutes until nicely brown. Remove and let sit 5–10 minutes. Cut into fourths and enjoy.

Meat, Fish, and Poultry

Believe it or not, the country of Italy leans slightly more to a vegetarian bent than to a meat lovers' tendency—unlike the United States. The Italian concept of meat, fish, and poultry is that it be small in portion, highly flavorful, and only one course—the secondo—out of many equally important courses served during the main meal.

The Italians' understanding of moderation in this sense is certainly commendable, as is their ability to create such mouthwatering, classic dishes. Where would we be without ossobuco and chicken cacciatora? So simple—so good.

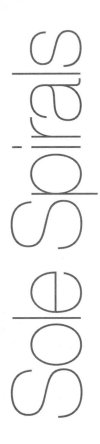

Sole Spirals

Serves 4:
8 thin sole fillets (about 3 ounces per slice)
4 anchovy fillets in oil
1 onion
2 cloves garlic
5 tablespoons olive oil plus oil for the baking dish
2 tablespoons grappa liqueur (optional)
2 tablespoons bread crumbs
4 bay leaves
Salt (preferably kosher or sea)
Freshly ground black pepper
4½ ounces fresh mozzarella
½ cup fresh parsley sprigs
3–4 sprigs fresh oregano
¼ cup fresh lemon juice

Prep time: 50 minutes
Per serving approx: 446 calories
43 g protein/26 g fat/8 g carbohydrates

Rinse sole fillets and pat dry. Finely dice 2 fillets. Drain and finely chop anchovies. Peel onion and garlic; chop both finely.

In a pan, heat 2 tablespoons of the olive oil. Add and sauté onion and garlic briefly. Add the diced fish, chopped anchovies, and whole bay leaves; sauté 2 minutes, stirring. Add grappa and bread crumbs; season with salt and pepper, and transfer to a mixing bowl. Remove and discard bay leaves.

Preheat oven to 375°F. Cut remaining fillets in half lengthwise to make 12 pieces total. Top each with a little of the sautéed fish mixture. Drain fresh mozzarella, cut into paper-thin slices, and lay one on top of each strip. Top each with freshly ground pepper.

Roll up fillet pieces. Place side by side in a large, greased baking dish.

Rinse parsley and oregano and shake dry; remove from stems and chop finely. Combine fresh lemon juice and remaining oil in a small bowl and whisk vigorously until cloudy. Stir in herbs. Season oil mixture with salt and pepper and drizzle over the sole spirals.

Bake spirals on the middle rack for 20 minutes and until fish is opaque throughout.

Mussels in Herb Wine Sauce

Serves 4:
6½ pounds live mussels
1 carrot
1 onion
4 cloves garlic
2 stalks celery
¾ cup fresh basil or parsley sprigs
1–2 sprigs fresh thyme (or ¼ teaspoon dried thyme)
2 tablespoons olive oil
2 canned whole peeled tomatoes
2¼ cups dry white wine
1 bay leaf
Salt (preferably kosher or sea)
Freshly ground black pepper

Prep time: 45 minutes
Per serving approx: 308 calories
18 g protein/10 g fat/14 g carbohydrates

Rinse live mussels under cold water and scrub if necessary. Throw away any that remain open.

Peel carrots, onion, and garlic, and rinse celery. Finely chop those four ingredients. Pull off basil leaves (or parsley) and chop. Rinse thyme and strip off leaves.

In your largest pot, heat oil. Stir in chopped vegetables and sauté briefly; stir constantly. Add herbs. Finely chop tomatoes and add along with wine. Add bay leaf, season with salt and pepper, and bring to a boil.

When boiling, throw in the mussels, cover, and keep the heat on high. Wait 8–10 minutes. Don't uncover, but occasionally shake the pot back and forth to shift the mussels.

Remove lid and look at the mussels. Most of them should be open. If a large number are closed, boil for another 2–3 minutes. After that, throw away any that are still closed. Remove and discard bay leaf. Serve open mussels in the cooking liquid. Add more chopped herbs, salt, and pepper to taste.

Basil-Saffron Fish Fillets

Serves 4:
1 yellow bell pepper
1 tomato
2 cloves garlic
¾ cup fresh basil sprigs
5 tablespoons olive oil
½ cup fish stock (or vegetable stock)
1½ pounds fish fillets (e.g., sole, cod, or halibut)
Salt (preferably kosher or sea)
Freshly ground black pepper
Several threads saffron
2 teaspoons fresh lemon juice

Prep time: 40 minutes
Per serving approx: 338 calories
33 g protein/20 g fat/5 g carbohydrates

Rinse bell pepper, halve, and discard stem and contents; dice rest. Rinse tomato and dice finely. Peel garlic and mince. Rinse basil, pull off leaves, and set aside. Coarsely chop stems.

In a pot, heat 2 tablespoons of the oil. Sauté bell pepper, basil stems, and garlic for a couple minutes, stirring. Add diced tomato and stock. Reduce heat to medium; simmer uncovered for 10 minutes. Bell pepper should be soft.

Meanwhile, rinse and pat dry fish fillets. Sprinkle both sides with salt and pepper.

Purée the sauce finely with a hand blender (or blender). Stir saffron into a little hot tap water and add to sauce. Season to taste with salt, pepper, and lemon juice.

In a large pan, heat remaining oil. Add fish fillets and sauté for one minute, then turn carefully (with a thin metal spatula) and cook for 1 minute (longer for thicker fillets—until opaque throughout).

Cut basil leaves into fine strips—stir into sauce or use as a garnish. Transfer fish fillets to four plates (preferably pre-warmed in a 170°F oven), top with sauce, and serve.

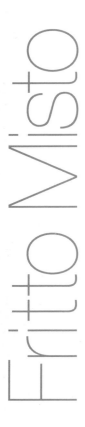
Fritto Misto

Serves 6:
¾ pound squid (preferably small tubes and tentacles)
Salt (preferably kosher or sea)
¾ pound raw, peeled, and cleaned shrimp
1 pound fresh sardines (specialty market)
1¼ pound other small fish or fillets (e.g., red mullet, small fillets of sole, or other white fish)
6 baby onions
6 marinated artichoke hearts
3 stalks celery
Freshly ground black pepper
½ cup flour or more as needed
4½ cups olive oil (NOT extra virgin)
3 lemons

Prep time: 1½ hours
Per serving approx: 727 calories
61 g protein/39 g fat/37 g carbohydrates

Rinse squid. Immerse for 30 seconds in a pot of boiling salted water. Rinse with cold water, drain, and pat dry.

Rinse shrimp and fish. You can leave the heads and fins on sardines and any other tiny whole fish. Rinse and pat dry fish fillets.

Peel baby onions and leave whole. Remove artichoke hearts from the jar and drain. Rinse celery, trim ends, and cut stalks crosswise into 1½-inch-long pieces.

Dust everything with salt and pepper. Spread flour on a large plate and, using two forks, turn each piece of fish and seafood until coated lightly on all sides with flour. Then repeat with the vegetables.

Pour oil into your largest pot. Heat until very hot (use oil thermometer and keep to around 350–375°F). Set oven to 170°F and warm a large oven-safe platter in it.

With a metal utensil, add as much fish and vegetables to the hot oil as can fit side by side. Squid and shrimp take 2–3 minutes, fresh sardines about 3 minutes, large red mullets 4 minutes, and thicker fish fillets about 5 minutes. Deep-fry vegetables until they take on a nice golden color. Remove cooked pieces with the metal utensil and drain briefly over the pot. Transfer everything to the warmed platter, lined with paper towels. Garnish fritto misto with fresh lemon wedges.

Veal Saltimbocca

Serves 4:
8 thin veal cutlets (about 3 ounces each)
1 tender baby zucchini
4 large slices prosciutto
16 fresh sage leaves
¼ cup butter
6 tablespoons dry white wine
Salt (preferably kosher or sea)
Freshly ground black pepper

Prep time: 30 minutes
Per serving approx: 395 calories
37 g protein/24 g fat/1 g carbohydrates

Set oven to 170°F and warm up an oven-safe plate or platter (for keeping meat warm later). Press cutlets flatter with the heel of your hand.

Rinse zucchini, trim ends, and slice thinly lengthwise. Trim slices to the length of the cutlets. Cut prosciutto slices in half.

Top each cutlet with 1 zucchini slice, 1 prosciutto slice, and 2 sage leaves; fasten to the meat by threading with a toothpick.

In a large pan, melt 2 tablespoons of the butter but don't let it brown. Add 4 cutlets with the topped side down; let cook over medium heat for 2 minutes. Turn and cook for up to 1 minute more. Transfer to the platter in the oven. In the rest of the butter, sauté all the cutlets in the same way.

Pour wine into the pan and stir with a wooden spoon to loosen the particles stuck to the bottom; simmer briefly. Season cautiously with salt and pepper (the prosciutto is already salty). Top cutlets with wine sauce and serve immediately.

Neapolitan Pork Chops

Serves 4:
4 pork chops, not too thick (or cutlets)
Salt (preferably kosher or sea)
Freshly ground black pepper
4 sprigs fresh marjoram or oregano
4 cloves garlic
1 (14-ounce) can whole peeled tomatoes
¼ cup olive oil
½ cup red wine
1 tablespoon tomato paste
1 tablespoon capers (optional)

Prep time: 50 minutes
Per serving approx: 494 calories
27 g protein/37 g fat/8 g carbohydrates

Pat chops dry and season on both sides with salt and pepper. Rinse and dry herbs, strip off leaves, and tear any large leaves in half. Peel garlic, cut in half, and then slice thinly. Chop tomatoes (reserve juice from can).

In a pan, heat 3 tablespoons of the oil. Sauté chops on both sides at high heat until lightly browned; remove and transfer to a plate. These will be cooked more later.

Pour remaining oil into pan. Stir in garlic and sauté briefly. Add herbs, tomatoes (and their juice), wine, and tomato paste; combine well. Season with salt and pepper, and simmer uncovered for about 5 minutes to reduce the sauce slightly.

Place chops in the sauce and spoon a little sauce over the top. Reduce heat, cover, and simmer for about 15 minutes. Garnish with capers if desired, and serve.

Meatballs in Red Wine Sauce

Serves 4:
4 slices sandwich bread
½ cup milk
2 ounces prosciutto
¾ cup fresh parsley or basil sprigs
1⅓ pounds ground meat (preferably half beef, half veal—ground by butcher)
1 tablespoon capers (optional)
2 tablespoons freshly grated Parmesan
Salt (preferably kosher or sea)
Freshly ground black pepper
1 medium onion
1 carrot
1 stalk celery
3 tablespoons olive oil
1 (14-ounce) can whole peeled tomatoes
¾ cup plus 2 tablespoons dry red wine
About 10 sage leaves

Prep time: 1 hour
Per serving approx: 696 calories
37 g protein/46 g fat/25 g carbohydrates

Remove and discard crust from bread; place rest in a shallow bowl with milk. Chop prosciutto finely. Rinse parsley or basil and chop leaves finely.

Squeeze liquid from bread, and break into small pieces. Combine in a bowl with ground meat, prosciutto, herbs, capers, and Parmesan. Season with salt and pepper, and knead until the mixture holds together. Roll bits of the meat mixture between your hands to form into the size of golf balls.

Peel onion and chop finely. Peel carrot, rinse celery, and dice both finely. In a large pan, heat oil. Sauté onion, carrot, and celery briefly, then push to the side and add meatballs. Sauté balls until brown on all sides.

Purée tomatoes along with their juice and the red wine (with blender or hand blender); add to the pan. Stir in sage, reduce to low heat, cover, and simmer for about 30 minutes. Season sauce to taste with salt and pepper—serve with meatballs!

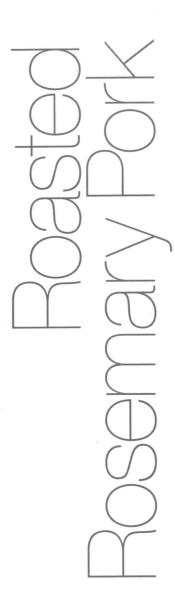

Roasted Rosemary Pork

Serves 6:
4 sprigs fresh rosemary
1 large lemon
4 cloves garlic
1–2 teaspoons fennel seeds
Salt (preferably kosher or sea)
Freshly ground black pepper
Freshly grated nutmeg
6 tablespoons olive oil
2½ pounds pork roast (boneless, fat trimmed, preferably tied into shape by butcher)
1 cup dry white wine

Prep time: 2½ hours
Per serving approx: 435 calories
29 g protein/31 g fat/3 g carbohydrates

Rinse rosemary. Remove needles from 2 of the sprigs. Rinse lemon, dry, and remove a thin layer of zest and chop. Peel garlic.

Pile rosemary needles, garlic, lemon zest, and fennel seeds on a board and chop all finely together. Combine that mixture in a small bowl with salt, pepper, pinch of nutmeg, and 2 tablespoons of the oil. Pat meat dry and rub mixture into it on all sides. You can either cook the roast immediately or let stand for a couple hours (refrigerated).

Preheat oven to 350°F.

Heat a large roasting pan, preferably cast iron. Add remaining oil. Brown roast well on all sides. Then place the roasting pan in the oven on the bottom rack. Add whole rosemary sprigs. Roast for 45 minutes (uncovered), then pour in wine. Cook another 1¼ hours or a bit longer for a larger roast, occasionally basting with wine and turning. Check the internal temperature of the roast with a meat thermometer—pork should be cooked to 170°F. Let stand 10 minutes before slicing.

Ossobuco

Serves 4:

For the meat and sauce:

4 slices veal shank (with center bone, each about 7 ounces)
3 carrots
2 onions
3 cloves garlic
3 stalks celery
½ cup fresh parsley sprigs
2 tablespoons butter
2 tablespoons olive oil
Salt (preferably kosher or sea)
Freshly ground black pepper
1 (14-ounce) can whole peeled tomatoes
About 1 cup beef stock

For the gremolata:

1 lemon
¾ cup fresh Italian parsley sprigs
2 cloves garlic

Prep time: 2½ hours
Per serving approx: 431 calories
45 g protein/19 g fat/20 g carbohydrates

Rinse meat slices with cold water and check for bone splinters; remove any. Pat dry.

Peel carrots, onions, and garlic; rinse celery. Chop those four ingredients finely. Rinse parsley, shake dry, trim stem end, and chop.

In a large casserole, dutch oven, or roasting pan, heat butter and oil. Brown meat slices on high heat, on all sides. Remove; season with salt and pepper.

In the same pot, sauté chopped vegetables and parsley briefly. Chop tomatoes and add to pot along with juice from the can and the stock. Turn heat down to medium and reduce liquid, for about 20 minutes.

Return meat to the pot, laying each side by side and spooning sauce on top. Simmer, covered, on low for about 1½ hours until tender. Before serving, salt and pepper to taste.

Meanwhile, prepare the gremolata. Rinse lemon and pat dry. Remove a thin layer of zest, avoiding the white bitter part. Rinse parsley and pull off leaves. Peel garlic. Chop zest, parsley, and garlic together very finely. Transfer to a small bowl and place on the table for sprinkling over the meat.

Hunter's Chicken (Cacciatora)

Serves 4:
1 chicken (about 3 pounds), cut into 8 pieces
1 large onion
2 cloves garlic
1 carrot
1 stalk celery
¾ cup fresh parsley sprigs
4–6 sage leaves
1⅔ cups dry white wine
¼ cup white wine vinegar (preferably white balsamic)
Salt (preferably kosher or sea)
Freshly ground black pepper
2 ounces pancetta or bacon
2 cups mushrooms
¼ cup olive oil
1 (14-ounce) can whole peeled tomatoes
¾ cup fresh basil sprigs

Prep time: 1½ hours
Per serving approx: 626 calories
35 g protein/41 g fat/14 g carbohydrates

Rinse chicken well inside and out under cold running water. Pat dry and cut into 8 pieces using a sharp knife and poultry shears (or purchase pre-cut). Place pieces in a bowl.

Peel onion and garlic and chop both finely. Peel carrot, rinse celery, and chop both. Rinse parsley and sage and chop finely.

Combine onion, garlic, carrot, celery, parsley, and sage with wine and vinegar and pour over chicken pieces. Marinate refrigerated for 6 hours or, even better, overnight.

Afterwards, remove chicken pieces, drain (but reserve marinade) and season with salt and pepper. Pour marinade through a fine mesh strainer (reserve both the vegetables and the liquid). Dice pancetta finely. Remove and discard mushroom stem-ends. Wipe off mushroom caps with a paper towel; quarter.

In a large stockpot, heat oil. Stir in pancetta. Add chicken pieces in batches and brown well on all sides, then remove.

Add mushrooms and vegetables from the marinade. Chop tomatoes and pour with their juice into the pot along with ⅓ cup of the marinade (discard rest if any). Bring to a low boil. Return chicken pieces to the pot, reduce heat to low, cover, and stew chicken for about 35 minutes or more. Pierce chicken at the thickest point with a sharp knife. If it's done, the juice that runs out should be clear. Finely chop basil and sprinkle over the top to serve.

Serves 4:
1 roasting chicken (about 2¾ pounds)
3 lemons plus 1 for garnish
3 cloves garlic
1 sprig fresh rosemary, plus more for garnish
Salt (preferably kosher or sea)
Freshly ground black pepper
2 tablespoons butter

Prep time: 1¾ hours
Per serving approx: 418 calories
29 g protein/32 g fat/6 g carbohydrates

Rinse chicken well inside and out under cold running water and pat dry. Rinse 1 lemon and slice, then squeeze juice from the other two.

Preheat oven to 375°F. Peel garlic, cut into slices, and then strips. Remove rosemary needles. Pierce chicken skin several times with the tip of a knife but don't cut into the meat. Insert garlic sticks and rosemary needles inside the holes, poked under the skin.

Rub salt and pepper into chicken skin. Melt butter but don't brown. Combine with lemon juice and brush the lemon butter onto the chicken.

Place the chicken in the broiler pan (the bottom deep baking pan part). Place lemon slices both on top and in the cavity; roast on the middle rack for about 1 hour and 20 minutes, occasionally basting with more lemon butter. Toward the end, baste with the natural juices as well. Pierce the thigh and if juice runs clear, it's done. Also, you can test for doneness using a meat thermometer inserted into the thickest part of the thigh. Let stand for a few minutes. Meanwhile, cut up the lemon; use as a garnish along with some fresh rosemary. Carve chicken, serve, and enjoy.

Roast Leg of Lamb

Serves 6:
2 pounds ripe tomatoes
2 pounds potatoes
6 tablespoons olive oil
4 sprigs fresh rosemary
Salt (preferably kosher or sea)
Freshly ground black pepper
1 onion
5 cloves garlic
1 lemon
$3/4$ cup fresh Italian parsley sprigs
$3/4$ teaspoon crushed red pepper flakes
1 piece boneless leg of lamb (about $2^{1}/_{2}$ pounds)
$1/2$ cup bread crumbs
2 ounces ($1/2$ cup) freshly grated Parmesan or pecorino

Prep time: $2^{1}/_{2}$ hours
Per serving approx: 638 calories
31 g protein/38 g fat/45 g carbohydrates

Core tomatoes and immerse in boiling water for 1 minute. Rinse under cold water, slip off peels, remove seeds, and dice. Peel potatoes, rinse, and cut into $1/3$-inch-thick slices.

Brush 1 tablespoon of the oil onto a broiler pan bottom. Fill with potato slices and top with diced tomatoes. Rinse rosemary, shake dry, remove needles, and sprinkle on top (reserve some rosemary for garnishing), along with salt and pepper.

Peel onion and garlic; chop both finely. Rinse lemon and dry. Remove zest and squeeze out juice. Rinse parsley, shake dry, and finely chop leaves.

Preheat oven to 350°F. Rinse lamb under cold water and pat dry. Trim away any fat. Mix onion, garlic, lemon zest, lemon juice, parsley, and pepper flakes with 2 tablespoons of the oil. Rub mixture into the lamb on all sides; season with salt. Place atop the potatoes. Cook on bottom rack of oven for $1^{1}/_{2}$ hours. Turn lamb once halfway through.

Increase temperature to 425°F. Combine bread crumbs, Parmesan, and remaining oil. Spread paste over lamb and cook for another 15 minutes or until golden.

Remove lamb from oven, cover with foil, and let rest 10 minutes. Then transfer to a board and slice. Garnish with fresh rosemary; serve slices with the potatoes and tomatoes.

Desserts

A dessert course at lunch in Italy is most likely to be, simply, a piece of fresh fruit. But more elaborate sweets certainly have their place in the Italian culture as well. Usually, a wedge of torta di cioccolata or other cake is enjoyed alongside espresso either in the morning or as a snack in the very late afternoon.

Also, it's a constant debate whether Itally originally invented ice cream. Whatever the case, we are surely indebted to Italians for the worldwide spread of unrivaled gelatos and flavored ices.

Tiramisu

Serves 6–8:
1⅔ cups strong espresso or coffee
1 large lemon
12 ounces (1½ cups) mascarpone
6 ounces (¾ cup) crème fraiche or sour cream
⅓ cup milk
½ cup sugar or more to taste
1 teaspoon vanilla
7 ounces ladyfingers
2 tablespoons grappa (or other liqueur)
1 teaspoon cocoa powder
1 pinch cinnamon

Prep time: 30 minutes
(+ 8 hours refrigeration time)
Per serving (8) approx: 411 calories
6 g protein/25 g fat/41 g carbohydrates

Make espresso or coffee and let cool (boiling water mixed with espresso powder works well).

Rinse lemon and dry—remove zest and squeeze juice from half. Combine mascarpone with crème fraiche, milk, sugar, and vanilla in a mixing bowl. Using whisk attachment on mixer, mix until cream is smooth. Stir in lemon zest and 1 tablespoon fresh lemon juice. Adjust sugar to taste.

Cover the bottom of a 9-inch square pan (2-inch-high sides) with a layer of ladyfingers. Combine espresso and grappa and drizzle onto the ladyfingers, or brush on. Soak as uniformly as possible.

When nice and coffee-colored, spread on one-third of the creamy mixture. Cover with another layer of ladyfingers and drizzle with liquid—then cream, then ladyfingers and liquid, ending with a layer of cream.

Finally, combine cocoa powder and cinnamon and dust the tiramisu using a fine mesh strainer. Refrigerate covered for at least 8 hours. Cut into squares and serve.

Panna Cotta

Serves 4:
1 vanilla bean
2 cups plus 2 tablespoons heavy cream
¼ cup sugar
1¾ teaspoons powdered gelatin
Butter for greasing ramekins (unsalted)
3 ripe peaches
1 tablespoon powdered sugar
2 tablespoons Amaretto
1 tablespoon fresh lemon juice

Prep time: 25 minutes
(+ 6 hours refrigeration time)
Per serving approx: 285 calories
3 g protein/21 g fat/21 g carbohydrates

Slit open vanilla bean lengthwise and fold out the two halves. Scrape out black seeds with a small paring knife and add to pot with vanilla bean, the 2 cups cream, and sugar.

Heat mixture. When it starts to boil, reduce heat and simmer for about 10 minutes. Meanwhile, in a small cup or bowl, stir powdered gelatin into the 2 tablespoons of cream—allow to soften for about 3 minutes (the last 3 minutes that the cream is simmering). Whisk gelatin mixture into cream mixture and keep stirring until completely dissolved.

Grease four individual ramekins or molds (⅔ cup capacity) with unsalted butter.

Let cream cool slightly, then pour into ramekins; let cool to room temperature (an hour or more) and then refrigerate for 6 hours or until firm enough to reverse onto a plate.

Meanwhile, make the sauce. Rinse peaches and halve. Remove and discard pits, and dice rest. In a pot, heat peaches with powdered sugar and Amaretto. Cover, reduce heat to low, and simmer for 10 minutes until soft. Let cool and purée with a hand blender or blender (or keep as is). Mix with fresh lemon juice.

Run a thin knife blade around the edges of the panna cotta to loosen. Cover with an upside-down plate and reverse quickly. The panna cotta should slide out onto the plate. Pour peach sauce all around.

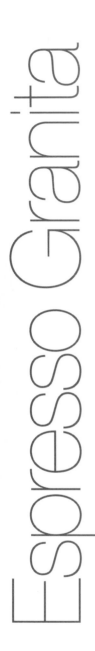

Espresso Granita

Serves 4:
2 cups plus 2 tablespoons strong espresso (or strong coffee)
⅓ cup sugar
3 teaspoons cocoa powder
½ teaspoon vanilla
1 tablespoon Sambuca liqueur (optional, or other coffee-type liqueur)
1 pint strawberries (as small and flavorful as possible)
1 tablespoon powdered sugar

Prep time: 30 minutes
(+ 4 hours freezing time)
Per serving approx: 80 calories
0 g protein/0 g fat/18 g carbohydrates

Make espresso (instant espresso powder mixed with boiling water works, too) and dissolve sugar and 1 teaspoon of the cocoa powder in it while still hot. Stir in vanilla and also the sambuca if desired.

Let espresso mixture cool. Take out a metal bowl that fits in your freezer. Pour in espresso and freeze for about 4 hours, stirring well once per hour.

Carefully rinse strawberries and pinch or cut off stems, and slice. Combine powdered sugar and remaining cocoa.

Divide granita into portions and transfer to small cups, glasses, or bowls. Place strawberries on top or serve on the side. Sift cocoa mixture over the strawberries. Time to enjoy!

Lemon Ice

Serves 4:
1 cup sugar
4 lemons
Small mint leaves

Prep time: 30 minutes
(+ 4 hours freezing time)
Per serving approx: 138 calories
1 g protein/0 g fat/38 g carbohydrates

Pour sugar into a pot with 1 cup water. Slowly bring to a boil while stirring constantly. Simmer liquid over medium heat for about 10–12 minutes until it becomes syrupy and a very pale golden color, to create a syrup. Let cool.

Meanwhile, rinse lemons, dry, and remove zest. Squeeze out lemon juice. Take out a metal bowl that fits in your freezer.

Stir lemon juice and zest into cooled syrup and pour into metal bowl. Place bowl in the freezer and freeze for about 4 hours. Stir at least once per hour, or more—the more often, the smoother it will be.

Distribute lemon ice in glasses and garnish with mint leaves, plus additional lemon slices if desired.

Torta di Cioccolata

Fills a 10-inch round cake pan:
7 ounces dark chocolate couverture (specialty baking store)
⅔ cup pine nuts
½ cup butter, plus 2 teaspoons butter for the pan
4 eggs
¾ cup sugar
1 teaspoon vanilla
⅓ cup flour
Powdered sugar and cocoa powder for dusting

Prep time: 1½ hours
Per serving (8) approx: 424 calories
8 g protein/34 g fat/31 g carbohydrates

Cut up couverture and melt over a double boiler, stirring frequently. Remove from heat and cool to room temperature.

Chop pine nuts very finely. Preheat oven to 300°F.

Separate eggs, with whites in one bowl and yolks in another.

In a mixing bowl, combine butter, sugar, and vanilla; beat until creamy (use electric mixer). Add egg yolks one by one and beat only until incorporated. Mix in melted chocolate a little at a time, then do the same with the flour (sift it in), then the pine nuts.

Beat egg whites with whisk attachment or an electric mixer until slightly stiff (make sure beaters/whisk are exceptionally clean and dry).

Fold a bit of the egg whites into the batter to soften it. Then pile the rest of the whites on top and fold in gently until incorporated.

Pour mixture into pan, using a rubber spatula to scrape the bowl clean. Bake on the middle rack for 45–50 minutes, or until a toothpick inserted near the middle of the cake comes out clean. Remove from oven and let stand for about 15 minutes. Take it out of the pan and let cool on a rack before cutting. Sift powdered sugar on top, cut, and serve.

Crispy Cherry Crostata

Fills a 10- or 11-inch round cake pan:

For the dough:
2 cups flour, plus more if necessary
⅔ cup finely chopped almonds
1 pinch salt
⅓ cup sugar
½ cup plus 1 tablespoon cold butter
1 egg
1 egg yolk

For the filling:
1¾ pounds fresh cherries, pitted
½ cup sugar
1 pinch ground cloves
1 lemon

For brushing:
1 egg yolk
1 tablespoon milk

Prep time: 2½ hours
Per serving (8) approx: 394 calories
8 g protein/21 g fat/46 g carbohydrates

Combine flour, almonds, salt, and sugar in a bowl. Cut butter into cubes; add along with egg and egg yolk.

Mix briefly, then knead on a work surface until mostly smooth (add a bit of flour if sticky) and you no longer see bits of butter. Form dough into a ball, wrap in waxed paper, and refrigerate 1 hour.

Meanwhile, prepare filling. Rinse cherries and remove stems. Pit with a cherry pitter.

Heat cherries, sugar, and cloves. Simmer uncovered on medium-low for 15 minutes. Rinse lemon and dry. Grate zest finely; add to cherries.

Preheat oven to 350°F.

Divide dough into thirds and set aside one-third. Knead the two-thirds together and form into a ball. Place the ball between 2 sheets of plastic wrap or waxed paper. Roll out into a thin circle slightly larger than a 10- or 11-inch cake pan. Remove the top sheet, reverse dough into ungreased pan, and remove other sheet of plastic. Press dough into pan, forming a 1-inch-high edge all around; pierce several times with a fork.

Roll out the one-third dough thinly between plastic sheets, and cut into strips. Spread stewed cherries atop dough in pan. Lay dough strips on top of the cherries, about 1 inch apart. Then rotate pan and lay on perpendicular strips to form a grid. Mix together egg yolk and milk; brush onto top dough strips. Bake on middle rack for 45 minutes, until top is golden. Let stand for 10 minutes in the pan, then remove and cool on a rack.